Belonging to the personal golf library of

GOLF IS A VERY SIMPLE GAME

THE GOLF TEACHINGS
OF THE LATE
SEÑOR FRANCISCO LOPEZ
VOL. I

Jonathan Fine

Published by Stand Tall International Inc.
124 Eglinton Ave. West
Suite 220
Toronto, Ontario
M4R 2G8

(416) 489-6600 or 1-888-FINEDEN (phone)
(416) 489-0036 or 1-888-KKAMODO (fax)

Copyright © 1996 Stand Tall International Inc.
All Rights Reserved

Printed and distributed by

Brown Book Company (BBC) Limited
720 King Street West
5th Floor
Toronto, Ontario
M5V 2T3

(416) 504-9696 or 1-800-463-5432 (phone)
(416) 504-9393 (fax)

Without limiting the rights under the copyright reserved above, no part of this publication may be reproduced, stored in or introduced into a retrieval system, if transmitted in any form or by any means (electronic, mechanical, photocopying, recording or otherwise), without the prior written permission of Stand Tall International Inc.

ISBN 0-9681882-0-6

CONTENTS

Chapter   **Pages**

1.	Introduction	1-4
2.	Golf Is A Very Simple Game:	5-6
3.	What Business Are You In?	7
4.	Why Do You Play Golf?	8-9
5.	Rent Or Buy?	10-11
6.	Play *Your* Game: Only Do What *You* Do Well	12
7.	Decisions, Decisions	13
8.	Where Can I Buy The Book?	14-15
9.	Look for What's Right with Your Game: Build On Your Strengths	16-17
10.	Build A Strength	18-20
11.	Come Into The Green From The Same Spot	21
12.	Be Quiet It Happens!	22-23
13.	Easy Bogey Golf	24-25
14.	Two Clubs And A Putter	26-27
15.	Make Every Hole A Par Three	28
16.	You Only Need One Great Shot Per Hole	29-30
17.	Stand Tall, Be Proud Like A Matador!	31-32
18.	A Matador Better Be Committed	33-34
19.	A Committed Golfer Cannot Fail	35-36
20.	Enthusiasm, Respect and Tolerance	37
21.	Is A Matador Afraid?	38-39
22.	You Are What You Think You Are: No More, No Less	40-41
23.	The Computer Within	42-44
24.	Who Does A Matador Blame?	45-46
25.	It's Not Fair	47
26.	Concentration	48

Contents

Chapter

Pages

27.	Keeping Your Focus	49-50
28.	Golf Is, "What Is". Over And Over Again	51
29.	Golf Is A Mental Game	52-53
30.	Think Good. Feel Good. Be Good	54-57
31.	I Am The Greatest!	58
	(So How Could I Hook It Into The Woods?)	
32.	Don't Think Of Me	59-60
33.	Think About What You Want To Do	61-62
34.	I Can Afford A Double Bogey	63-64
	And Still Score...	
35.	Automatic Golfer	65
36.	Play Every Hole Like You've Never Played It	66-67
37.	Sounds Like A Plan	68
38.	Getting Ready To Hit The Ball	69-72
39.	Do I Have To Do This Routine Every Day?	73
40.	What Club To Hit	74
41.	Practicing	75-76
42.	Chipping	77
43.	Putting Practice	78
44.	Putting	79-80
45.	Must Shots	81
46.	Chipping Practice	82
47.	Videotaping: What Are You Doing Right?	83
48.	Make Love To Your Golf Course	84
49.	Try Walking Your Course Green To Tee	85
50.	Make Your Own Course Book	86
51.	The Rules	87-88
52.	There's More Than One Way To Play A Hole	89
53.	Tournament Match Play	90
54.	Hang Tough And Steady	91-92
55.	Be Emotionally Neutral	93-94
56.	Dominate Your Opponent	95-96

Contents

Chapter   **Pages**

	Chapter	Pages
57.	It's Over When It's Over: Not Until	97
58.	Go With What Got You There	98
59.	Play Good Enough To Win	99
60.	You Are Your Only Friend	100
61.	Forget The Score	101
62.	Tournament Medal Play	102
63.	Win Or Lose: Like A Man	103
64.	Get Your Butterflies Flying In Formation	104
65.	The Zone	105-112
66.	Be Happy, Juan	113-114

My wife *Shelley* and my kids *Corby*, *Jamie*, *Jory* and *Jake* for their love and support, *Frankie Lopez*, *The Emilio Lopez Family*, *Gabriella Lopez* for the cover design of the first printing of this book, *Jesse Dylan* and *Tony Daniels*, *Bob Brown* for his technical advice and support in the publication of this book, my partner *Mario Deo* for his friendship, *Friends and Family all*, *Steve Justein*, *Phil Taylor*, *Peter Kirsch*, *Brian Hennick*, *Jack Pappalardo*, *Albert Doria*, *Ken Shaw* and *Ralph Gileno*.

Graphic Images contained in the following commercial packages:

1.   Presentation Task Force
        Publisher's Task Force
        by
        New Vision Technologies Inc.

2.   Word Perfect Suite
        Corel Gallery
        by
        Corel Corporation

3.   PC Paintbrush Clip Art Collection
        by
        Softkey International Inc.

cover photograph: Frank Lopez as a 15-year-old caddy in Spain

cover design: Paedric O'Sullivan

FORWARD

I *have seen the future, and you're not in it!*

Those were the words from Jonathan Fine as we sat by the pool at our golf club, two days before our semi-final match for the club 'B' championship. Needless to say, Jon beat me 4 and 2 on his way to the championship, chipping in on the first hole for a birdie on a downhill-sidehill chip.

This would not be such a big deal except that in one season Jon completely turned his game around, and I don't recall ever seeing him practicing at the range. The previous year, Jon would muddle his way through and struggle to break 90. His drives were errant and his short game was nonexistent.

In 1996, Jon was a man possessed. I have never seen anyone look as focused as he did. It was obvious that he had a new approach to the game of golf. He had a new pre-shot routine that he used religiously and his short game was awesome; in fact, uncanny at times. He exuded confidence as he walked down the fairways and was simply unflappable.

At the beginning of the season I had to give Jon six strokes in our friendly matches, by season's end, we were playing even and breaking eighty. I asked Jon what he attributed his great improvement to. He smiled and asked me if I had known the late Frank Lopez. I said that I had not. Jon told me that I would soon find out all about Frank when he finished writing the book of Frank's teachings.

Jon gave me an advance copy of *Golf Is A Simple Game: The Golf Teachings of the Late Señor Francisco Lopez* and I can tell you that it had an *immediate and most profound impact* on my game.

I used to dread standing on the first tee, worrying that a poor first drive would destroy my round. I would often come apart if I hit one poor shot during a round. Now I have discovered a new pleasure in golf. My confidence is improving with each shot and I feel for the first time that I am in control of my game.

Unlike other golf literature that is highly technical or primarily aimed at very low handicap golfers, this book made me feel good about the skills that I already have and how to get the most out of them. I was thrilled to read a book that a double-digit handicapper can use and not get all caught up in technical mumbo jumbo.

You made the right choice in buying this book. Guard it closely. Your golfing friends will want to borrow this book from you - forever!

Play good golf!

Steve Justein
Tournament Chairman
Oakdale Golf and Country Club
Toronto, Ontario

1

INTRODUCTION

Francisco (Frank) Lopez was both my golf teacher and my friend. I first met him in 1974 shortly after I started playing golf. He gave me a wonderful gift - a passion for the game of golf, and the advice that golf was simple and fun.

With Frank's guidance, my handicap dropped rapidly, but, rose just as quickly after he left our club to pursue his career elsewhere. My game was so bad in fact, that there was a joke around the club that anyone who wanted to play with me ought to do it by the end of June, because that's when I quit each year.

Over the years we kept in touch, and whenever my golf got so bad that I couldn't stand it, I would meet Frank at the driving range and he would straighten me out in three minutes-literally!

All that changed suddenly.

On Thursday, March 26th, 1992, I received a telephone call.

"Juan?"

"Frankie, how are you?"

"Why don't you come over to my house for lunch. I want to talk to you."

"I'm in the middle of a trial for the next couple of weeks. I'll call you in a couple of weeks."

" I won't be here in a couple of weeks."

"So, call me when you get back."

"Juan, two weeks ago the doctors tell me I have four weeks to live."

I put down my work and rushed over to Frank's house.

Frank was obviously ill. Although he was tanned and as well groomed as ever, he had lost what appeared to be at least 50 or 60 pounds.

After telling me the details of his impending death, we reminisced. Strange as it may seem, we joked that he would come back after he was dead and continue to help me with my golf. We watched the videotape of our match at Glen Abbey the year before and in the middle of the tape, he turned it off so he could show me how I wasn't *tourning* my back to the hole enough. That was Frank. He loved the game of golf. And he loved to teach it.

As I was leaving after the first of many visits, Frank gave me several keepsakes, perhaps my most treasured possessions today. Then he told me to come back in a couple of days for a special gift.

I visited Frank many times over the next week or so and on what turned out to be my last visit to him, he sat me down and said, *"Juan, you remember we talked last year about making a teaching video?"*

"Yes, I remember."

"Well, we won't be able to do that now. So, what I do for you was to make you a tape recordings of some things that I been telling you for almost 20 years. Take this gift from me to you and do with it whatever you want."

"Thank you, Frank."

Frank Lopez died April 9th, 1992. Frank's brother, Emilio, told me that Frank played an imaginary round of golf, sat down in a chair, looked up in the air, smiled, said *"Open the door"*, and died.

Much of this book is a lightly edited transcription of the tapes given to me by my friend Frank Lopez, interspersed with remembrances of his teachings over almost 20 years and my thoughts. As the book is written as Frank speaking to me, I have chosen not to use any quotation marks. As well, in places, I have tried to capture Frank's pronunciation and grammar. [I have also noted some of my first-time listening reactions in square brackets and a different font.]

As you will no doubt realize, Frank's
philosophy of golf (and by the way, of life) was to experience
it with passion, simplicity,
wonderment and honour.
Dive in, get wet and love it.
In fact, <u>*The Golf*</u>
<u>*Teachings Of The Late*</u>
<u>*Señor Francisco Lopez*</u>
are really as much about
life as they are about
golf.

Frank Lopez teaches us that playing the best golf that you can possibly play requires commitment, respect, trust, courage, love, pride, humility, tolerance, enthusiasm, unwavering belief, tenacity, honour, discipline, undaunted devotion and self-confidence. In short, *live your life and play your golf with excellence.*

You are probably wondering whether *your* game will improve if you follow Frank's simple approach to the game of golf. The best way that I can answer that question is to tell you what following *The Golf Teachings Of The Late Señor Francisco Lopez* did for *my* game.

I started transcribing the tapes and writing this book in the fall of 1995, at which time my handicap was 18. I followed *The Golf Teachings of the Late Señor Francisco Lopez* this season; my handicap dropped to a 12, I broke 80, something I hadn't done in almost 20 years, and I won the "B" flight Club Championship at my club. All of this without hitting more than one large bucket of balls at the range throughout this time.

Will *The Golf Teachings Of The Late Señor Francisco Lopez* do anything for your game?

"That's up to you, my friend."

Jonathan Fine
November, 1996

2
GOLF IS A
VERY SIMPLE GAME

Juan, do you know what your biggest problem is?

[That's a nice way to start!]

You think too much. But not *just* too much, you think about the wrong things!

Golf is a very simple game, but many people try to make it complicated. Some teachers get involved with things like swing planes, wrist angles and torque. Too complicated. So much to think about, it distracts you from what you got to do.

Last time you came to see me, you were hitting the ball like your grandmother! How long it take me to get you hitting the ball well again? Three minutes or two? What I tell you, Juan? *Stand tall, be proud, and hit the ball.* That's all it took to get you to crunch them long and straight. You were even hitting your driver with your eyes closed!

Keep it simple Juan. Master the simplicity of the game. Golf is a very simple game. Simple.

If you want to shoot the best scores that you can possibly shoot, only one thing matters: *getting the ball into the hole in the fewest number of strokes.* That's what *playing* the game of golf is all about.

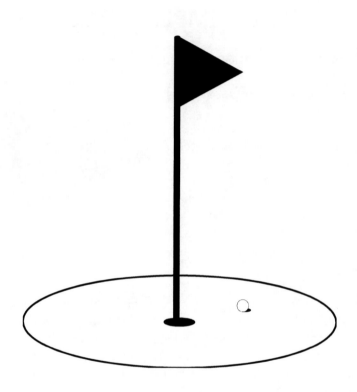

**Get the ball into the hole
taking the fewest number of strokes.**

3

WHAT BUSINESS ARE YOU IN?

I tell you a story. When I first came to Canada I played in a tournament and I played with a guy who hold the club with his hands in a baseball grip. This guy have a terrible looking swing and used old and dirty clubs. You know what? He shoot 68 and beat me. I couldn't believe it but this guy understand the game of golf.

Get the ball into the hole taking the fewest number of strokes.

He didn't care that he had an ugly swing. He didn't care that he didn't look like a golfer. He didn't care about anything else but putting the ball in the hole. When he got close to the green, he was deadly. This guy putt with a miniature golf course putter. Juan, I tell you, I never seen anything like it. This guy shoot the ugliest 68 I ever seen, but when they asked him his score, they didn't ask 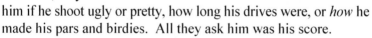 him if he shoot ugly or pretty, how long his drives were, or *how* he made his pars and birdies. All they ask him was his score.

Accuracy is what counts, not style or strength. When you play golf, you got to make a decision what business you are in and then get down to business.

When you play golf, you are in the business of
putting the ball into the hole
in the fewest number of strokes.

4

WHY DO YOU PLAY GOLF?

I teach so many people in my life and I see people play golf for all different reasons. Why do you play golf?

[I began to think. There are many reasons why I play golf on any particular day. I know I play golf because I like to play golf but then again, some days I hate the game and still play it.

I guess one thing that drives me is the thought that maybe today will be the day that I play well, score well, hit beautiful straight and long drives.

What are other reasons that people play ...?

So you can tell your friends about your round?

To see how far you can hit the ball, how many fairways you can hit, how few putts you can take, how few balls you can lose or how many balls you can find?

To see if you can go a whole round without duffing a shot?

To get a hole in one? To win a match? To win some money? To entertain a business associate? To get some exercise? To get rid of frustrations? To get frustrated?

Wow. On any given day, we can have a multitude of reasons for playing!]

I know you been thinking because I asked you a question which makes you think. Golf is such a great game that there are many, many good reasons to play. Whatever your reason, remember this: *golf is a game. Play it. Have fun.*

You don't "work" the game of golf, you "play" it.

If you don't have fun playing golf, do something else.

5

RENT OR BUY?

I remember one day many years ago when I first started teaching you. You were a good student and you improved quickly. I laughed one day when you came to me and said, *"Frank, I've got it. I've got it. I've finally got it. I own this game!"*

Do you remember what I say to you, Juan?

I say to you, *"You never own it. The best you can ever hope to do is just rent it for a while."*

Every day I play I think to myself, *"Señor Lopez, what swing you bring today? What clubs you going to hit sweet? How you going to be chipping and putting today?"*

It's the same for every golfer. Every golfer.

In golf, just because you learn how to do something and you do it once, doesn't mean that you can do it always.

In golf, if you learn how to do something once and then you do it, all you know is that you've learned how to do it and that you've done it. Once.

But that's the point.

You know that you can do it because you've done it.

Juan, golf is like life in many ways.   In golf and in life, your success is determined by the quality of your bad shots. You take what you get and you have to do the best with it. Sometimes "Life Is" hitting a par five in two and four putting from three feet. Sometimes "Life Is" hitting three worm-burners to the edge of a par four and chipping in for par.

You will not hit the ball perfectly every time. No one can do that.   But you can play *excellent* golf.

Excellent !

Making excellence your goal leaves room for errors and for success.

You have a good basic swing. *Trust it and use it!* So get up there and *hit the ball.*

Playing golf is what happens after you hit the ball.

Some days you will have it and some days you won't.   Some days you will be able to putt, but not hit off the tee. Some days you will be missing two footers, but crunching them off the tee.

Playing golf means being able to adjust the way that you play based upon what is and isn't working for you and finding a way to score well, even if it's one of those days!

6

PLAY *YOUR* GAME:
ONLY DO WHAT *YOU* DO WELL

Y ou got to play *your* game. You can't play my game or anyone
else's game. Play *YOUR* game.

What does that mean, *play YOUR game?* It means *only do what
YOU can do well.*

This is so important that you should think this every
time you make a shot. Every decision that you make
on the course should be with only one
thought in mind. You know what that is?

[Let's see Frank, could it be the
same thing you've told me five
times already in the last five
minutes?]

That's right!

How YOU, Juan Fine, get the ball into the hole in
the fewest number of strokes.

Play YOUR game. Only do what YOU can do well.

7

DECISIONS, DECISIONS

Every shot that you take is important, but the consequences of making a bad shot on certain shots, are more severe than on others. On these types of shots, it is *critical* to use the proper club or to land in the proper position. The difference between making the right decision and the wrong decision could be two strokes or more.

Play a round of golf in your mind and figure out how many of these types of shots you would have to make in an average round on your course.

Are you finished?

I bet you that there are probably about 25 of these shots.

It's the decisions on these shots
that make the difference
between good scores and bad scores.

8

WHERE CAN I BUY THE BOOK?

So how can you make the right decisions? I know you are thinking that there must be a book that you can buy to help you make these decisions.

[This guy knows me a bit too well.]

There is no book and there are no rigid rules because the right decision is different for each person.

There is only a pool of knowledge and experience, called *your* subconscious, that *you* can draw on to achieve *your* purpose, which is *getting the ball into the hole in the least number of strokes.*

Your subconscious is like the shy, class genius. It has a library of distances, conditions, temperatures and wind speeds and it will *announce* the correct club to use *if you ask it.*

The more information that you give it, the more accurate and reliable your subconscious becomes. Just like the class genius, it is constantly computing, figuring and reworking the answer so it will be the first to get the right answer if asked. This is why it's important to be aware of as much as possible on the golf course at all times.

Make a conscious effort to consider factors such as wind, stance, lie, distance and temperature before *every* shot. This gives your subconscious a better opportunity to give you an accurate and reliable answer to your questions.

Use the time that you are *not* playing a shot to gather and process as much information as you can. Be aware of the hardness or softness of the fairways and the greens, the difference in texture of certain greens or bunkers to others, how the other players' shots fly, whether their shots are short or long, whether their shots are affected by the wind, the roll of their putts at the beginning, in the middle and at the end of the putt, and on and on. This is all part of *playing* the game of golf.

Once you finally consult your subconscious, go with the first choice. That will usually be the right choice, so trust it.

You got to learn to trust it.

9

LOOK FOR WHAT'S RIGHT
WITH YOUR GAME:
BUILD ON YOUR STRENGTHS

One thing that I try to teach you is to *look for what's right with your game*, not for what's wrong. If you look for what's wrong, then you are focusing on negative thoughts. As long as you focus on negative thoughts, you cannot play the best golf that you can possibly play.

I hear many people tell me that they need to *fix their game*. To fix something, it must be broken. To *believe* that you need to fix something, means that you must *believe* that it is broken.

These people are focusing on what they *believe* to be broken about their game. In other words, they are looking for what's wrong with their game. They are searching for and focusing on negative thoughts.

16

How can you play the best golf that you can possibly play if you believe that you are playing with a broken swing?

Forget about *fixing* your game. Juan, trust me, it's never going to be perfect.

Look for what's right in your game.
Play the game of golf with what you got.

One of the greatest thrills in golf is scoring well when part of your game isn't working. If you are constantly thinking about fixing your game, you'll miss some of the most satisfying games of your life.

Think about what your strengths are and build on them.

You know what shots you are good at. You know what clubs you have more confidence in. Everybody has parts of his game which are better than others and everybody knows what they are.

Plan your game around your strengths.

Trust them and rely on them.

They are your friends.

If you don't have any strengths, build some. Then put yourself into a position where you can plan your game around these strengths.

10

BUILD A STRENGTH

There will be many greens that you can't reach in regulation. If you can't make the green in regulation, don't try. Accept it. Don't fight it. But this doesn't mean that you can't par the hole.

Sure you can! That's called *playing* golf!

Your job is to *find a way* to get the ball into the hole in the fewest number of strokes. Your job is to *find a way* to par the hole even if you can't reach the green in regulation.

So how are you going to this, Juan?

Build a strength.

One reason that golf is such a great game is that it is really many different games in one: the long game, the sand game, putting, the short game...

I'm talking now about *the short game.*

The short game is the scoring game.

You are playing the short game when you are within about 50

yards of the green.

The next time you play, keep track of the number of shots, including putts, that you take from inside 50 yards. You'll see how important the short game is. I'll bet you that around half of your strokes are taken from within 50 yards of the green.

Half of your strokes, Juan. *Half of your whole game is played from within 50 yards!* What does that tell you?

[Uh, let's see Frank. Could it be that the short
                    game is very important?]

That 50-yard area is where you either score or don't score.

Check your scorecard next round. I'll bet you'll see that the difference between an average score and a career round will be six to 12 putts that didn't drop or chips that weren't tight. That's how important the short game is.

Juan, I tell you that the average golfer can make golf such a simple game. If you *believe* that you can get up and down in two or less from inside 50 yards, then you take pressure off yourself on your approach shots, which takes pressure off yourself on the tee.

You got to have one club in your bag that you know inside out for shots up to 50 yards. You got to know that if you get within 50 yards of the green, you can put the ball not just on the green, but close to the pin. If you do this, *you can plan each hole around that club.*

If you can't get to the green in regulation, then put yourself in position on the fairway so that you can go into the green with the club in which you have the most confidence.

For example, let's say you have a 390-yard par four. You could hit two 150-yard irons and be 90 yards or so from the pin. If your favourite club was your wedge, you could then hit it stiff, or at least on the green so that you would be putting for par.

The point that I am getting at is that sometimes, for example, your second shot on a par five may be a wedge that puts you 150 yards from the hole because a lower club may pose a risk or put you in no better position.

***Build a strength,
and then build your game
around your strength.***

11

COME INTO THE GREEN
FROM THE SAME SPOT

I want you to play a practice round where your aim is to come into the green on every hole from the same distance inside 100 yards, give or take 10 yards (unless of course that will put you out of bounds or in a hazard). Practice this and you will *know* that you can get onto the green from that distance.

Notice how your confidence increases. You *know* you can get the ball onto the green from that distance. You *know* you can get the ball close.

What I want you to learn is at least one shot from a particular distance that you *know* you can make. I don't care if you use "the right club". I don't care if the shot looks pretty. I don't care if you will be embarrassed to tell your friends what club you used. All I care is that you have a shot that you can make from that distance *over and over again*.

12

BE QUIET IT HAPPENS!

I remember you telling me once how well you scored one day. You tol' me how well you were driving the ball off the tee and how many greens you hit, but how bad your putting was.

The next day you tol' me that you couldn't hit the ball off the tee and you didn't hit very many greens, but your chipping and putting was deadly. *You scored the same.*

The next day you were spraying them off the tee right and left, but you were scrambling out of your mind. Once again your short game came to the rescue. *You scored the same.*

I also remember the day after that when you tol' me that your driving was awful, you didn't hit any greens and your putting and chipping was even worse than your driving. *You scored very poorly that day!*

That's the way golf is. Even the games of the touring pros fall apart some days. What you have to learn is how to adjust when part of your game falls apart, and still score well.

Most days, if you use your head, you can *manage* your game so you can still go about your business and succeed.

Some days there's simply nothing that you can do about it.

13

EASY BOGEY GOLF

Here's a game that I want you to play one day. It's called *Easy Bogey Golf.*

Play a round of golf with the plan of playing a round of bogey golf. In other words, add one stoke to par on each hole and see if you can play Easy Bogey Golf.

Don't put any pressure on yourself for any shot. Nice and easy, every shot. *Keep the ball in play.* When you are playing Easy Bogey Golf, you aim for the middle of the green regardless of where the pin is. Those are the *only* thoughts for today.

You will probably not need a driver on any hole. That's good. In fact, you will probably be able to tee off with say a 5-iron on every par four and par five.

[Get real, Frank!]

That's right Juan, a 5-iron. Get out your calculator, I'll show you why.

Say you have a 420-yard par four. You hit a 5-iron say 160 yards. That leaves 260 yards to the middle of the green and 110 yards to the 150-yard marker and only 160 yards to the 100-yard marker. Play this hole 5-iron, 5-iron, wedge and see what happens.

I tell you what happens. You hit 5-iron off the tee, you are in the fairway. You hit 5-iron off the fairway, you are still in the fairway lying 100 yards from the middle of the green, maybe 80 yards from the front of the green. You can get on the green easily from 100 yards out so just aim for the middle of the green. You will be on the green in regulation for this game of Easy Bogey Golf and putting for par.

When you are playing Easy Bogey Golf, think only of lagging your first putt within a three foot circle of the hole. Maybe it will go in, maybe it won't, but I tell you that if you play every hole like this, you will train your mind how to recover from bad shots and bad days. If you sharpen your short game so that you can get up and down in two wherever you are around the green, you've got your bogey, maybe a par if you sink a chip or a putt.

Now let's say you are not playing Easy Bogey Golf, but you are playing the same hole for score in a match. Par four, 420 yards. All but the best golfers would have to put two of their best, very best shots together, back-to-back, to expect to get there in two.

Think of the pressure that you put on yourself to hit two of your best shots back to back with the second one probably being an accurate long iron or a fairway wood.

Why take a chance of a double or triple bogey when you know that if you play Easy Bogey Golf on this hole, the worst that you will probably do will be to get a bogey. Two 150-yard shots, however, will put you within 120 yards of the green and you ought to be able to put your third shot on or close to the green. You'll be surprised how many times you put your third shot "gimme-close" or drain your putt for the par.

14

TWO CLUBS AND A PUTTER

Y ou remember when you were called in a match for carrying 15 clubs?

[Now I do.]

Why you carry so many clubs? You know you're only allowed to carry 14 clubs. Can't you count, Juan?

Well, you don't even need 14 clubs. As a matter fact, I want you to play a round of golf with two clubs and a putter.

[Two clubs and a putter?]

That's right, two clubs and a putter.

Which clubs will you choose?

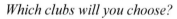

Try to choose clubs that you don't use that much. For sure you need a club for distance, but will you choose a wood or a long iron? I think you choose a long iron because a wood won't help you if you get into deep rough or in a tight lie. *So, which long iron will you choose?* Probably 3-iron for because you need distance, but you can also choke down on a 3-iron or punch it if you need something less than a full 3-iron shot.

For the short club, I think you choose a 9-iron because it has a nice combination of distance and loft to give you the most options on the course.

When you play this way the first time, don't keep score. Just think of this round as a driving range on wheels. Take one shot at a time and just try to make the best shot that you can.

Above all, keep the ball in play. See if you can go a whole round without having to play anywhere but from the fairway or a green.

There will probably be many greens that you can't reach in regulation. That's OK and that's the point of this game. You will be able to make each green in one over regulation.

Get out your calculator again, Juan. Say you hit a 3-iron 180 yards. 180 + 180 = 360, which puts you within 9-iron distance of any par four. 180 + 180 + 180 = 540, which puts you within 9-iron distance of any par five, if not on.

Even if your 3-iron distance is 160 yards because of a mis-hit or wind, you can still make any green in one over regulation. 160 + 160 = 320, which still puts you within 9-iron distance of just about any par four. 160 + 160 + 160 = 480, which puts you within 9-iron distance of just about any par five.

I bet you will notice that without the pressure of trying to make the green in regulation, your swings will be easy, smooth and flowing. Because you use the wrong club on just about every shot, I bet that you will be more aware of each shot and how to make it. You will learn how to adjust your game to the circumstances, how to improvise to get the job done. You will train yourself to think about how to get the ball into the hole with the least number of strokes.

15

MAKE EVERY HOLE A PAR THREE

H ere's something else that you can try.

If you ask the average golfer what are the easiest holes to play, par threes, par fours or par fives, what do you think most people will say?

Par threes. So once you get within striking distance of the green, think about the rest of the hole as a par three.

Try this on every hole and see what happens.

16
YOU ONLY NEED ONE GREAT SHOT PER HOLE

How many times I tell you: *Keep the ball in play?* It's so important.

You only need one great shot per hole. If you are not going to get where you would like to go on the next shot, play an absolutely guaranteed safe shot.

So, on a par four, if your drive doesn't leave you a good shot to the green, accept that your second shot is *not* going to be your great shot on this hole. You still have two opportunities of making that one great shot you need on that hole. Sometimes you will and sometimes you won't, but at least you have given yourself the opportunity to do so.

Put yourself in position so that your third shot can be your great shot on that hole. If your third shot isn't great, you still have a chance to make your fourth shot, your great shot on that hole and par the hole.

When you are going for the green, unless you are at your favourite distance from the green, always consider going for the centre of the green, unless there is good reason to aim somewhere else.

Sometimes, it's better to play just short of the green if, for example, the green slants towards the fairway and the pin is at the front. What would you rather have a short uphill chip and a putt, or a long downhill putt, and then who knows what after that?

Pace out all of the greens on your course. You will see that they average about 20 to 40 yards in length. If you aim for the centre of the green, you can mishit your shot by 10 to 20 yards short or long and still be putting. If you aim for the pin in the front or the back and mishit the same way, you are off the green.

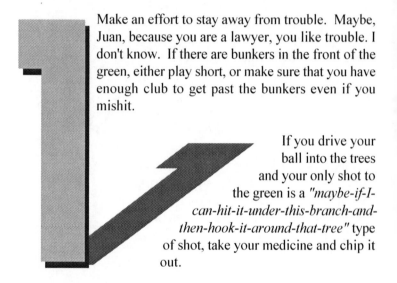

Make an effort to stay away from trouble. Maybe, Juan, because you are a lawyer, you like trouble. I don't know. If there are bunkers in the front of the green, either play short, or make sure that you have enough club to get past the bunkers even if you mishit.

If you drive your ball into the trees and your only shot to the green is a *"maybe-if-I-can-hit-it-under-this-branch-and-then-hook-it-around-that-tree"* type of shot, take your medicine and chip it out.

If *this* shot isn't going to be your great shot on the hole, play it so you give yourself the best chance of making your *next* shot, the great shot on the hole.

Making a par after chipping out of the trees can destroy an opponent.

Taking a double or a triple bogey after hacking your way out of the woods can destroy your game.

You only need one great shot per hole.

17

STAND TALL, BE PROUD LIKE A MATADOR!

You know I tell you many times "Stand tall, be proud like a matador, and hit it!"

You know why I tell you this? The matador stands in the *plaza de toros* and faces a huge bull with sharp horns. Many matadors before him have been gored and even killed, but each matador faces each bull with *valor*, pride and courage.

Just like a golfer thinks about putting the ball into the hole in the least number of strokes, the matador thinks about killing the bull with grace, style, courage and dignity. *Triunfo total!*

The matador faces *death* every second, but he stands tall and proud, all the time! He knows that he could get gored or die. He is a matador. It goes with the job. He doesn't worry about what *could* happen, because that takes his mind off what he has to do.

At one time or another, every golfer experiences fear, sometimes almost panic. But why? The worst that a golfer faces when he stands up to a ball is a duffed shot, a missed green, a slice or a hook, a hazard or out of bounds. Of course, that could happen because you are playing golf. That's *the game* of golf. Duffing, slicing, hooking, out of bounds, lipping out are all part of what can happen when you play the game of golf.

But why think about all of those bad things? If they happen, they happen. Then you have to do something about them.

That's the game of golf.

But, just like the matador, it's much better to think about what you have to do.

18

A MATADOR
BETTER BE COMMITTED

*H*ow long do you think a matador would last if he wasn't sure
that being a matador was what he really wanted to do?

Not too long.

Do you think a matador think to himself, *"Maybe I should be a
picador?"*

No way. A *matador de toros* think of only one thing: being a
matador de toros.

Once he makes that decision, everything
about being a matador just seems to
fall into place. He dresses in his
traje de luces. He wears his hair in a
coleta. He gets all the *avíos de
matar* he needs to kill the bull: a
muleta and an *estoque*. He thinks
about being a matador. He is
known as a matador and pretty
soon he finds himself at the
plaza de toros opposite a bull in
a *corrida de toros*, none of which
would happen if the matador hadn't
first *made the decision* to be a
matador.

33

The *same thing* happens when *you* make a decision, a promise to yourself, to play the best golf you can possibly play. A *commitment* to play the best golf you can possibly play.

When *you* make a commitment to play the best golf you can possibly play, *it becomes important to you* to play golf well. You start trying to find ways to do this. *How do you do this?* You practice, you read golf books and magazines, you watch golf tournaments, you talk about golf with your friends and with the pro at your club, you dream about golf, you hang around with golfers and eventually you are known as and you become a person who is interested in playing better golf. Pretty soon people start approaching you and asking you questions about this and that.

Once you make the commitment, the mental decision to play the best golf that you can possibly play, *something magical seems to happen.*

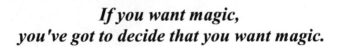

You become a magnet for all that is golf and you *will* play the best golf that you can possibly play.

Don 't ask me how it happens, I don't know. Maybe soon I'll know. All I can tell you now is that *it does happen.*

**If you want magic,
you've got to decide that you want magic.**

19

A COMMITTED
GOLFER CANNOT FAIL

There is no such thing as failure to a golfer who is committed to playing the best golf that he can play. It's possible for such a golfer to slice, hook, duff, shank, even whiff *and still be committed* to playing the best golf that he can possibly play. You see Juan, being committed to playing the best golf that you can possibly play doesn't end as soon as you make a bad shot.

```
[Commitment to playing the best golf you can possibly
play is a journey: it's not a destination.

Commitment to playing the best
golf you can possibly play is a
process: it's not an event.]
```

Golf is a game of facing and overcoming one obstacle after another. Golfer against the course. Some obstacles you will overcome. Others you won't. *Commitment* to playing the best golf that you can possibly play means that you remain committed, *regardless* of the obstacles that you face.

To a committed golfer, failure is *not* an option. *It doesn't exist.* It's impossible. *Every shot is what it is and then it's time for the next shot.*

You may slice drives, you may shank approach shots, you may miss short putts. That's part of the game of golf to which you are committed. Once you are committed to playing the best golf that you can possibly play, you can deal with all of these things when they happen, *as just being things that happen when you play golf.*

If you are *not* committed to playing the best golf that you can possibly play, you might experience the same bad shots as further evidence that you are a bad golfer and give up on the hole and the round.

Part of what can make you a good golfer is *believing* that you are a good golfer. See yourself as a good golfer and you will come to expect good shots. Bad shots will be aberrations, mistakes, not you.

> **If you believe that you are a good golfer,**
> **a poor shot is simply a poor shot.**
> **But not, a typically poor shot.**

If you think that a poor shot is simply a poor shot, you can detach yourself and your ability as a golfer from the shot. You can say to yourself, *"Oh, that's not me. That's just a bad shot. I have to expect some bad shots. Fortunately, I've got one or two more chances to make a great shot and make par or bogey.*

Do you see the difference?

20

ENTHUSIASM, RESPECT AND TOLERANCE

Commitment to playing the best golf that you can possibly play generates

enthusiasm,

respect

and tolerance,

all of which you need to play the best golf that you can possibly play.

21

IS A MATADOR AFRAID?

*D*o you think the matador who is staring el toro in the eyes, is afraid?

Of course the matador is afraid! Who wouldn't be afraid standing alone in the *plaza de toros* by himself facing an angry bull? Even so, the matador still goes about his *brega*, his business, and does what he has to do even though he is afraid.

You see Juan, the matador knows that fear is only in your mind. It's only a prediction of what could happen. It's your mind worrying about the future.

Just like the matador, it's possible for you to go about your business on the golf course with courage and honour, and still be afraid.

You can be *aware* of the danger areas and even be afraid of them, and still golf effectively. You can be afraid, but *not notice* the fear, because you prefer to go about your business with courage and dignity. It's like having pain and taking a pain pill. The pain is still there, you just don't notice it.

The matador only have one opponent. The bull. In golf, you have many opponents, or so it seems some days. The golf course. Yourself. Your opponent. The weather. Divots. Soft fairways. Hard greens. The wind. The rough. Bunkers. Water. All of these opponents make every shot you ever take different from every shot you have ever taken, or will ever take. Each one of these opponents can affect your shot but, *sooner or later, you've got to take the shot!*

Why not simply stand tall, be proud like a matador, and hit it?

Just before you hit your ball, do you know *exactly* where it is going to go? Of course not. You may have a pretty good idea, but even the best golfers in the world hook and slice their drives, or hit them shorter or longer than expected.

You never know *exactly* where your ball is going to land, so why worry about it? Why concern yourself with this thought? *Just stand tall, be proud like a matador, and hit it.*

How many times have you parred a hole after a bad drive? How many times have you bogeyed or double bogeyed a hole after a great drive? It happens to everyone.

No one can predict accurately the outcome of any shot in advance. Everyone has doubts and fears about his or her ability on any given day and on any given shot. Everyone is capable of making shots above or below his or her ability level.

Why not simply stand tall, be proud like a matador, and hit it?

22

YOU ARE
WHAT YOU THINK YOU ARE:
NO MORE, NO LESS

*Y*ou know why the matador always stand erguido, tall and proud?

Because the matador knows that *how you think determines how you act.*

You can't possibly be a good golfer, if you don't think that you are a good golfer.

The best that you can perform is to the level of your own expectations, but no better.

At any ability level, those golfers that score better, *believe* that they can do it. *These golfers believe that they can do it.* That's it. They expect to do it and are surprised, but not disappointed, if they don't.

Think about it for a minute. *If you want to improve, then you have to play beyond what you believe your current ability to be.* If you never play over your head, you'll never get to be a better golfer.

Being committed to playing the best golf that you can possibly play means always believing that you can play beyond what you believe your current ability level to be.

Be proud of yourself when you play over your head.

It means that you are improving.

Isn't that what you are trying to do?

Pretty soon what used to be "playing over your head" will become "your game" and playing over your head will take you up to a new level.

23

THE COMPUTER WITHIN

I quit school when I was very young, but I learned a lot of different things in my life about the way our bodies and our minds work.

Just like your body, *you must train your mind* to think properly.

Your mind operates at different levels. For example, there is the conscious level, the subconscious level, etc. There's another part of your mind that remembers every shot that you have ever made. There's another part of your mind that likes to make excuses. There's another part of your mind that will try to adjust and compensate for every bad shot that you have ever made.

Your subconscious is like a computer, always being programmed and re-programmed by what you think and experience.

The subconscious does what it's told. It doesn't make judgments. If you tell it that you are a good golfer by talking to yourself, by seeing these thoughts in your mind, by carrying yourself in that manner and by talking to others about this, it will believe you and it will switch into that mode. On the other hand, if you think that you are a bad golfer, if you act like a bad golfer, if you walk, talk or think like a bad golfer, your subconscious will switch into "bad-golfer" mode.

You can tell your subconscious how you want things to be and then it will go out and do it. It will process information according to how it is programmed, because unlike you, your subconscious has *complete and reliable discipline.* Your subconscious is always working, always processing information, never making judgments.

Your subconscious aims to please. It is your servant, but once you set it loose, it is your master. In other words, *you can program your subconscious to be any way you want to be, but once you do, that's the way you will be.*

That's why to be a good golfer, you must think that you are a good golfer. You must *train* all parts of your mind to think like a good golfer.

The matador knows that he can program his subconscious by thinking good thoughts.
He knows that a person who is *courageous, dignified and respectful* of his opponent, stands tall and proud, and so he stands tall and proud. He knows that if he carry himself with *confianza*, self- confidence, then he will be *self- confident.*

When you stand tall and proud, it tells everyone and everything, including your subconscious and the golf course, that you are a dangerous foe, that you intend to go about your business, that you will meet any obstacle, any impediment, any hazard or any situation with *strength, pride, dignity and tenacity* and that you will not let anything get in the way of your business, which is trying to put the ball into the hole in the least number of strokes.

When the matador walk into the *plaza de toros*, does he walk in with his head down looking at the ground? Does he wear dirty old clothes? Does he rush around and act impulsively? No. He *parades* with *honour, pride and dignity.*

Have you ever noticed how good golfers take pride in their work? How they take what they do seriously enough to be deliberate and not to rush?

When *you* walk down the golf course, *parade* like the matador making the *paseo* into the *plaza de toros*.

Walk with *pride.*

Walk with *purpose.*

Walk with *excitement and anticipation.*

Walk with *brió, brilliance and vivacity.*

Walk like you've got a rope attached to the top of your head that I am pulling from heaven.

24

WHO DOES A MATADOR BLAME?

The matador, he never make excuses. Who's he going to blame? The matador knows that if he makes a mistake, it was he who make the mistake and it is he who has to bear the consequences.

Making a mistake doesn't mean that you are a bad golfer. Every golfer, even the touring pros make mistakes. Playing the best golf that you can possibly play is playing the shot that will minimize your mistakes, minimizing the damage if you do make a mistake, and dealing with the mistakes that you make.

Golf is perhaps the only game where you don't play against a person. Even in a head-on match, *you play against the golf course.* You don't have to worry about the strategy of your opponent - the course. You don't have to worry about the actions of your opponent - the course. All you have to do is to get the ball into the hole.

If you hit your ball into a hazard, it was you that hit the ball into the hazard. It wasn't your opponent, the course, that caused you to hit the ball into the hazard or that strategically deflected your ball into the hazard.

Do you see what I am saying, Juan?

The course is just there and everything that happens on the course is the result of what you do.

Just like the matador, you must learn to accept that *everything that happens on the course is the result of what you do.*

**Take responsibility
for what you do on the course,
and
take control of your game.**

25

IT'S NOT FAIR

Golfers who don't accept responsibility for what they do like to blame others. One of their favourite expressions is, "It's not fair".

I don't understand this.

Is there a book somewhere which tells you what a fair pin placement is? Is there a book somewhere which tells you how fast the greens should be? You take the course as you find it. That's the whole point of golf.

Master the course as you find it.

The golfer who can put the ball into the hole in the least number of strokes on the course of the day, wins.

So what if the pin is cut into the side of a side-hill down-hill slope? Everyone plays the same course.

Take the course as you find it, and play it.

26

CONCENTRATION

I remember you ask me how I can tell you just to stand tall, be proud, and hit it, when there are so many things to remember. I tell you that by the time you think of all of those things, you forget what you were trying to do.

Try this. Count to 60 and think of nothing else but the numbers that you are counting. See if you can get to 60 without any other thought entering your mind, including the thought whether you can get to 60 without another thought entering your mind.

Ready? Go. One, two, three....

```
[...four, five, six. This is really
stupid...seven... who couldn't
concentrate counting to 60 - oops.]
```

You can't do it. You can't keep your mind from wandering.

That's one of the things that happens when you stand over the ball too long.

So, what's the answer? It's simple.

Play golf!
Stand tall, be proud, and hit it.
Then start getting ready to do it again!

27

KEEPING YOUR FOCUS

No one can concentrate fully on only one thought for the four or five hours that it takes to play a round of golf. You can't do it because your mind is continually processing the information that it receives.

There is just so much going on and your brain is so complicated, that it is natural to drift out of focus or to lose your concentration. Expect this, because it will happen. The trick is to recognize when it is happening and then to get back into focus.

So, how can you do this?

I tell you. The first thing you have to know is what you want to be thinking about and that is only one thing: getting the ball into the hole in the least number of strokes.

Once your mind wanders on to some other topic, gently prefer to get yourself back into focus. Prefer to think the thoughts that you *choose* to think. Just slide back to where you want to be.

How can you do this? Simply smile to yourself and think about your next shot and how you can get the ball into the hole in the fewest number of strokes. Start assessing the situation for your next shot. The lie. Your stance. The wind. The placement of the pin. Trouble areas ahead. The distance to the hole, etc.

You don't need to be alarmed or get mad at yourself for drifting.

***Just gently resume focusing
on what you got to do.***

***Pretty soon you are back, focused
and playing golf.***

28

GOLF IS, "WHAT IS", OVER AND OVER AND OVER AGAIN

*W*hen you are deciding what club you are going to use, what do you think about?

It does not matter what club you used at this tee yesterday, that you usually hit a 5-iron 160 yards, that you once hit your tee shot into the woods or into the bunker on the right, or that you once got a hole-in-one here.

It does not matter that your opponent is using a 4-iron or that your partner is using a wedge, that you read that you *should* be able to hit a 5-iron 160 yards, that you *would* feel like a real wimp if you used your 4-wood or that you *could* afford a bogey and still break 80.

It does not matter! *It does not matter!* *It does not matter!*

Once you start thinking, *"I should be able to...I might be able to ...",* instead of, *"I know I can ...",* you are in trouble.

The only thing that matters is which club will assist you in achieving your objective of getting the ball into the hole in the least number of strokes.

29

GOLF IS A MENTAL GAME

I don't know what happens to people when they get on a golf course. I teach doctors, lawyers, judges, business people, architects...people that you think are really smart. But when they get on the golf course, often it's like they forgot how to think!

Golf is a mental game and that means many different things.

Juan, remember this:

think only good thoughts.

Don't dwell on the bad things that happen to you in life or in golf. They are over. They have happened. *Choose* to remember only the good things that happen to you. Always *prefer* to look at the good side of everything. And there is always a good side to anything. You must make a definite decision, *a commitment,* that you are going to do this and then train yourself to do it.

Be conscious of bad thoughts and of when you are thinking them. When this happens, just think a good thought.

I know it sounds simple but it is. And if you do it, you will see that it works. It's simple.

Train your mind to remember only the good things that happen.

This will assist you in keeping in mind what you want to do and giving you the confidence that you can do it.

Here's what I want you to do. Keep a notebook in your locker and after each round, keep track of *only the good things* that happened in that round. If you were putting well, mark it down. If you made a spectacular shot, write a detailed note about it in your book. Be proud of that shot and tell the whole story so that when you read it again, you will be able to relive the moment. That's what you are trying to do. Relive the good moments and train your mind to relive *only* the good moments.

Take 15 minutes before you play each day and read your favourite parts. Read your notes every night before you go to bed. Let your subconscious go to work while you are sleeping.

Give yourself a library of the best moments of your golfing career and your internal historian will remember you as a great golfer.

Golf is a mental game. You got to start training your mind to think only good thoughts.

30

THINK GOOD. FEEL GOOD.
BE GOOD.

There is so much that scientists don't know, but I tell you something that I learned just from watching people and believing what I see.

I can tell when my students are having a good day or a bad day. I can feel whether my students are thinking good thoughts or bad thoughts. I can tell when my students are going to have a good lesson or a good game.

You know how you meet someone and right away this person make you feel good, just being around them. There are also other people that you meet. Even without talking to them, you know that this person is depressing and you feel uncomfortable.

I believe that what you think about controls the type of energy that you emit: your personal energy field. In other words, if you think good thoughts, your energy field will be strong, bright, vibrant, jubilant and expanding, and will affect everyone and everything around you, including yourself, in a positive way.

If you think bad thoughts, your energy field will be depressing, constricting, dulling, and debilitating: an implosion of negativity which paralyses the spirit and makes the necessary frame of mind impossible.

If you feel good, then you will have confidence in yourself and your game. If you have confidence in yourself and your game, *then you will give yourself the best opportunity to play well and shoot a good score.*

This is why I tell you to stand tall, and be proud, like a matador. This is why I tell you to play your own game. This is why I tell you to only think about what you want to do. This is why I tell you to keep track of only the best things that happen to you.

If you feel good, then you give yourself the best opportunity to play well.

I see some people who are always in bad moods. *They never play good golf.*

I see some people who always seem depressed. *They never play good golf.*

I see some people who are very shy or who have no confidence in themselves. *They never play good golf.*

These people never enjoy themselves on the golf course, but it's not because they don't have the basic skills to play a good round of golf for their skill level. The reason they don't enjoy themselves is *only* because of what they are thinking about.

I tell you Juan, when I am dead, I will be wishing that I could have the chance to play my worst round of golf!

There is no reason not to be happy on the golf course. Golf is just a game. It make no sense to play golf and make yourself angry and unhappy. At the very worst, a game of golf is a four or five hour walk in a beautiful park with some friends. Exercise, fresh air, friendship, fun.

As you walk the course, *enjoy* the beauty of the golf course and the nature that is part of it. Feel the softness or the hardness of the fairways as you walk to your ball. *Observe* how different weather conditions affect the consistency of the bunkers. *Lose yourself in its splendour.*

Take a moment and watch the fox that lives on the course as it trots across the fairway. Think how *lucky* you are to observe the hawks sitting on the fairway trying to pick up your golf ball.

Be fascinated with the excellent condition of the golf course and the effort that it must have taken to obtain and maintain such a high level. *Be equally fascinated* with the poor condition of the golf course and the challenge facing you of how you will have to adjust your game to deal with those poor conditions.

Be amazed that of all the places on this huge fairway where your ball could have landed, it landed in a divot. Find it *interesting* that after practising 15-foot chip shots for 20 minutes prior to the round, you just put your 15-foot chip shot 40 feet past the hole. See this as an opportunity. If you always put your approach shots "gimme-close", you would never experience the thrill of draining a 40-foot putt.

Be intrigued with the thought that trying to keep all of your game together at any one time is like trying to contain a fistful of Jell-O.

Revel in the challenge that golf presents, shot after shot, after shot, after shot, after shot...

Be appreciative of your opponent, the starter, the back-shop guys, your partner, the other golfers on the course, all of whom in one way or another are part of this great event - namely you pursuing your commitment of playing the best golf that you can possibly play.

Enjoy competition for the thrill of it. *Can you be excited about competing in a match that comes down to the last putt on the 18th hole, win or lose?*

Understand and appreciate that golf gives us many opportunities for greatness. If your opponent sinks a long putt to make your next putt critical, be excited. He has given you an opportunity for greatness. Enjoy the moment and savour it, *regardless of whether you make the putt.*

Make a point of talking to yourself often and reminding yourself how lucky you are to have the opportunity to play your best round of golf. *Smile inwardly and outwardly.* If you do all of this Juan, you will put yourself in the right frame of mind to play the best round of golf that you can possibly play.

31

I AM THE GREATEST!
(SO HOW COULD I HOOK IT INTO THE WOODS?)

S o, what happens when you think only good thoughts, you think that you are the best golfer in the world, you remember only the best shots you have ever made, you think about where you want to hit the ball *and then you duff, shank it, slice it, hook it, miss a short putt ...*

You have a number of options. You can swear and throw your clubs. You can berate yourself for making such a stupid shot. You can vow that this will be your last round. You can concede the hole to your opponent. You can tell yourself that you can never get a par on this hole. You can give up trying.

OR

You can *understand and accept* that duffs, shanks, slices, hooks, apparently are part of your game that day, and then you can start thinking about your next shot, *looking forward with the excitement* of trying to recover, scramble and salvage your way to getting the ball into the hole in the fewest number of strokes.

32

DON'T THINK OF ME

Juan, as you sit here listening to my voice, don't think of what I look like.

Juan, I tell you *not* to think of what I look like! You can't do it, can you?

[So, what's the point, Paco?]

The same thing happen to you when you stand up over the ball and think about what you *don't* want to do. Many times you *do* what you *don't* want to do.

Your mind works with images of the target. When you think of a "possible" target, either where you want to go or where you *don't* want to go, it's like your mind takes a photograph of this "possible" target and interprets it as your intended target.

This is why taking a moment to stare at your target and visualize your shot helps you. It gives your mind a chance to get a clear, sharp image of where you want the ball to go. With practice and observation, you can almost feel your mind "lock-in" on the target.

But, when you think to yourself, "Don't hit it into the water", your mind sees an image of the water and the ball going into the water just like you thought of what I looked like when I told you not to. Your mind thinks you want to hit the ball into the water. It can't hear you thinking "Don't" hit it into the water.

***This is why it's so important
to think only about what you want to do and
where you want the ball to go.***

33

THINK ABOUT
WHAT YOU WANT TO DO

I remember one round we played many years ago. You had never broken 80, but had been close many times. I tol' you that you played well enough to break 80, but you didn't think you did.

Before this game, you tol' me that you had a game plan. *Keep the ball in play and go for the centre of the greens.*

After 17 holes, you needed a par on 18 [a par three] to come in with 78, your best score ever. As you stood up to the ball, I could see your thoughts suddenly shift from what you had to do, to your score and then, to what you didn't want to do. In your mind, you started adding up the score and I could see you *pleading with yourself* just to get a par so you could shoot 78.

But you didn't think that you deserved a 78 because you didn't think you were that good a golfer.

I could see you thinking: *don't hit the ball into the creek; don't hit the ball into the woods; don't hit the ball to the right; don't hit the ball into the bunker.*

You tol' me afterwards that you just repeated these thoughts to yourself over and over again. Then you calculated that even if you bogeyed the hole, you could still come in at 79. At worst a double bogey and an 80, which would have been your best score that year.

Then you swung and hit the ball into the creek!

You were so flustered by your thoughts that you must have been relying on sheer will to project the ball towards the hole. Experience tells us this does not work.

You hit your next shot short of the green, lying three. I could actually see you quickly doing the calculations in your head and realizing that if you holed out this blind uphill 75 yard shot, you could still reach your goal of breaking 80. Do you remember where this shot went Juan?

Into the bunker!

Once again you were calculating: five out and onto the green, sink the putt for a triple and come in at 81. You got out of the bunker and as you stood over the putt, you told me that you were thinking, *"Don't miss the putt, Jon, but what ever you do, don't three-putt!"*

Juan, three putts, an eight and an 83. Qué làstima! You ought to be ashamed of yourself.

You know what you said to me after that round, Juan?

You said *"Frank, 83. Not bad? Pretty good, actually. Just about what I figured I would score if I played really well. Boy, was I lucky today. Things just seemed to be going right. Played way over my head for most of this round. Next time I will probably break a hundred on the wrong side so that this success will even out."*

Guess what happened next time you played?"

 [Thanks for reminding me of that spectacular 102.]

34

I CAN AFFORD A DOUBLE BOGEY AND STILL SCORE ...

How many times you tol' me, Juan, that you stood on the 18th tee, six or seven over par and then you took a double, triple or quadruple bogey?

For 17 holes you were playing shot by shot and that got you to a position where you could break 80. Then you started thinking about the score. You weren't thinking about your shot. You weren't thinking about what you had to do. You were thinking about what you *wished* you could do. You were *wishing* that you would par the hole so that you could break 80. Why you do this? You don't "wish" the ball into the hole.

Thinking about the score is not going to help you get the ball into the hole in fewest number of strokes.

In fact, it will do the opposite.

If you play golf *one stroke at a time* with the sole objective of getting the ball into the hole in the least number of strokes, there is no need to think about your score until you walk off the 18th green because, up to that point, it doesn't matter.

When you are thinking about the score, you are thinking, "if this, if that", instead of thinking about the shot that you have to hit.

When you think about the score, you are thinking, "don't do this, don't do that", and then you do exactly what you thought you didn't want to do.

If you find yourself thinking about your score (and you will), it's OK. Simply get back to what you want to be thinking about.

35

AUTOMATIC GOLFER

S tanding on the tee is no place to think about *how* to hit the ball. When you are standing on the tee, you take a deep breath and *let the shot happen*. I call this automatic golfer.

Automatic golfer is a place that's just a bit different than the place where you *try* to make a particular shot. When you are in automatic golfer, your computer takes over and automatically sets the controls so that your muscles, bones, ligaments and tendons do what they are supposed to do. You are not thinking about the mechanics of your shot. *You know and you do.* It's the difference between *hitting* golf balls and *playing* the game of golf.

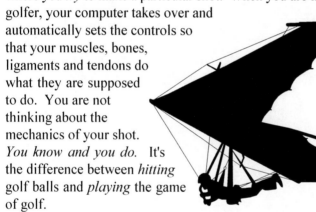

Let it happen .

36

PLAY EVERY HOLE
LIKE YOU'VE NEVER PLAYED IT

S ome people don't like playing new courses because they don't
know how to play each hole.

When you are standing on the tee playing a new course, you are
searching for the best way to play the hole, *not*
for various ways *not* to play the hole. All of
your thoughts are directed to *what you have to
do* as you figure out how you are
going to play that hole. You are
standing on the tee making a plan.

Often, when you stand up on the tee
at your home course, do you notice
that your thoughts are directed to what
you *don't* want to do?

Sure, because you have played the
same course hundreds of times and
you feel like you have played just about every
bad shot possible. You know those sports
bloopers tapes? When you think about all of the
bad shots, it's like watching a sports bloopers
tape of yourself. That will not build your
confidence; it will destroy it.

If you are driving in your car headed for Toronto, you don't say to
yourself, *"Juan, don't go to Montreal."* It's the same thing in golf.

Think about what you want to do with the ball.
Think only about where you want to put the ball.

Make a plan as to where you want to hit the ball,
and then stand tall, be proud, and
hit it.

Golf is a game of
planning your
shots, not just
hitting your
shots.

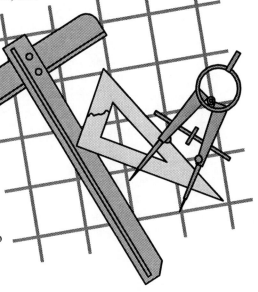

Playing golf means
planning where you want
the ball to go and *then*
hitting the ball to that
place, all with the overall
aim of getting the ball into
the hole with the least
number of strokes.

37

SOUNDS LIKE A PLAN

It's important that you do this exactly as I tell you. Get a notebook and number the pages one to 18. On each page make a sketch of the 18 holes of your course, including greens, fairways, bunkers and other hazards, labelling the distance and par of the hole together with the approximate location of the 200, 150 and 100 yard markers. Then, make three plans in different colours noting the landing spot of each shot and the club that you would probably use for each shot.

 For the first plan, plan how you would ideally play the hole so that you hit every green in regulation.

 For the second plan, plan how you would play each hole with the sole objective of staying in the fairway and out of the bunkers, trees and other hazards.

 For the third plan, plan to play each hole as if the par for the hole was one stroke higher. In other words, play a par three as a par four, etc. In this game, *you are not permitted* to be on the green until you are one-over regulation.

Once you have three plans for each hole, play three rounds trying to stay strictly to one of the plans each round. See what happens.

38

GETTING READY
TO HIT THE BALL

Juan, part of being committed to playing the best golf that you can play is being disciplined.

One thing that requires a lot of discipline is always doing the same thing before each shot or type of shot. Some people call this a "pre-shot routine".

I know you are asking, *"Why should I do a pre-shot routine?"* . I tell you why.

There are so many different things that can affect your performance on the golf course that it is important to eliminate as many as you can.

Having a pre-shot routine and the discipline to repeat it every shot, gives you something about your game that you can easily control.

You can make the first thing that you do on every shot constant and consistent. *Maybe, if you can make the first thing that you do on every shot constant and consistent, then you give yourself a better chance of being constant and consistent on every shot?* What you think?

Going through the same motions before you hit the ball has a number of advantages. The most important is that it is a trigger to remind your brain to give your muscles the correct instructions to hit the golf ball. It is a trigger for your brain to remember all of those previous successful shots which started off exactly the same way. It is a signal to your sub-conscious "automatic golfer" to take over.

You know how sometimes you stand up to the ball and it doesn't quite feel right? You feel misaligned or just not quite set up properly. In those circumstances, you may or may not execute the shot that you want, but either way it doesn't matter. Even if you make a good shot, you have no frame of reference to which your sub-conscious can attach that good shot . You think ,"how did I do that", and you try not to get into that same uncomfortable position again.

When you execute the same pre-shot routine, it builds up your confidence. You are telling yourself that you know the formula for hitting a good shot and it begins with this particular and specific pre-shot routine. The pre-shot routine subtly reminds you that you are committed to playing the best golf that you can possibly play.

The pre-shot routine is signal to your brain that you are ready to make a shot.

When you execute a good shot, your subconscious now has something that it can associate with that good shot. A pre-shot routine gets you into a comfortable and familiar place. It is the trigger that gets you into the zone.

By repeating the same thing that you have done thousands of times, it reminds your subconscious of all of the good shots that resulted and gets your mind off of the mechanics of hitting the ball.

Consistently doing the same thing puts you in a familiar place and there is a certain comfort in familiarity, which in turn gives you confidence and anchors you for the job at hand.

In match play, a consistent pre-shot routine tells your opponent that you are a steady, disciplined, determined and stubborn golfing machine.

So what should *your* pre-shot routine be? Create your own pre-shot routine, but I think it must have certain elements.

For drives, long shots and approach shots you must take at least one practice swing. I think you should take two. The first practice swing should be a baseball swing. This gets you turning your shoulders and hips, gets you behind the ball and releasing your hands. Then, take a golf swing like the one you will be taking.

Once you know the swing, stand behind the ball and pick an object in the distance, like a tree, a building or a power line. Face it squarely and tell yourself that you want to hit the ball towards that object. Wait for a moment while your mind locks in on the target. You will know when it does.

Keeping your eye on this target, walk up to your ball *always watching that target* and not the ball. Make a 90-degree turn still looking at the target and put your club down. You will be in the right position to hit the ball in the direction you want to go. Don't readjust your stance. *Trust it, Juan. Trust it.* If you are uncomfortable, then stand back and do the same thing over again.

When you are ready, take a deep breath and let it out, then stand tall, be proud like a matador, and hit it.

Let 'im go!

This routine is good because it forces you to think about where you want to go.

If you are on a hole where the tee box is not aligned square to your target, take a moment to let your mind adjust the way that it sees the hole so you get the feeling of being aligned square to the target. If you consciously make the decision that you want to perceive your alignment this way, and give your mind a chance to adjust, it will do it for you.

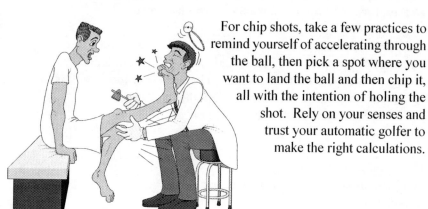

For chip shots, take a few practices to remind yourself of accelerating through the ball, then pick a spot where you want to land the ball and then chip it, all with the intention of holing the shot. Rely on your senses and trust your automatic golfer to make the right calculations.

39

DO I HAVE TO DO THIS ROUTINE EVERY DAY?

I know you are asking yourself whether you have to do your pre-shot routine before *every* shot, *every* time you play, right?

[Well, I mean for some shots...come on.]

Absolutely. Make it part of how you *play* golf. If you are playing golf, then *play* golf. If you *are committed* to playing the best golf that you can possibly play, then *be committed* to playing the best golf that you can possibly play.

If you do your pre-shot routine enough, you won't have to ask this question because it will become natural to you. *It will become the way that you play golf.* You won't be "doing it", it will just be *what happens when you play golf.*

What you need to do is to develop a pre-shot routine that works for you and repeat it over and over again on every shot until it becomes part of the way that you play golf. *It doesn't matter* if it's just a 3-inch putt. *It doesn't matter* if you've just put your drive out of bounds. *It doesn't matter* if you just birdied the last hole.

Every shot. Every day. It's the way you play.

40

WHAT CLUB TO HIT

*H*ow do you decide what club to hit?

If you give your mind the right information, you can sense the proper club to use. Pay attention to everything. Be immersed not only in your game, but in your playing partners' games as well. You can learn a lot from what they do.

As soon as you have hit your last shot, you should be thinking about your next shot, assessing the conditions and giving your mind as much information as possible. The more information you can give your mind, the better answer you will get when you ask what club you should use.

Be there. Right there. All the time.

Give your computer lots of information: the lie, the distance to the pin, centre of the green and trouble, your target, the wind, what's in front of, beside and behind the target.

Then, give your mind a few moments to tell you the right club to hit and yourself a few moments to receive the message.

Once you have the answer, go with it and trust it.

41

PRACTICING

To maintain or improve your skills, you must practice.

The key is WHAT do you practice and HOW do you practice. *Do you practice tee to green or green to tee?* In other words, do you start your practice rounds at the driving range, or on the putting green?

Most of us practice tee to green and often our practice doesn't take us past the tee.

I say do exactly the opposite.

Start your practice session on the putting green, putting and chipping. This gently eases you into the right frame of mind and body for playing golf. It warms up your brain, muscles and senses for scoring. You focus immediately upon getting the ball into the hole.

If you have time (and you should try to make some time), go to the range. The driving range is good for practicing what you have learned in a lesson. Often, however, we practice our bad swings or spend countless hours waiting for that perfect swing as if once we finally find it, we will be able to do it for all time.

Juan, if you are waiting to perfect your swing, you'll be waiting a long time. It's not going to happen.

Many golfers like to *"work on their game",* which really means practice their weaknesses. Not that you shouldn't take lessons and practice, but not on the course when you are going for score.

When you play a round where score matters, play your strengths.

Go with what got you there.

42

CHIPPING

I tol' you that your subconscious remembers every shot you have ever made, has a pretty good idea of the right feel for every shot that you will ever take, and will take care of things automatically.

When you are chipping, the first thing that you have to do is to decide what club you are going to use. Pretend that you see your ball being chipped onto the green, noticing in your mind's eye where it will hit and how it rolls into the hole, feeling how hard it would take to toss the ball to get it there. Take a couple of practice chips to get the proper feel of the club, then let your body go into *automatic golfer*.

You must trust that this will work Trust it.

Go for the hole. You are trying to sink your chips because the object of the game of golf is getting the ball into the hole in the fewest number of strokes.

You can do the same thing with long putts. Rely on your automatic golfer to judge the right distance and go for the hole.

43

PUTTING PRACTICE

I see so many different putting drills it can make you crazy just trying to remember all of them.

Here's three and these are all you need:

1.   For your short putts, line up five balls about six inches apart, starting about one foot from the hole. Stand beside the first ball and, without dwelling over each shot, make each putt. Remember: you want to hit each putt firmly like you are tapping a hammer. Practice this a few times, varying the distances between the balls.

2.   For your medium range putts, say three to eight feet, put five balls in a circle around the hole. See how many you can sink and then do it again using a different sized circle.

3.   For your long putts, look at the hole and call on your automatic golfer to hit the ball the right distance.

Practice these drills and you will be a good enough putter.

44

PUTTING

Stand tall and proud for every shot, even your putts.

The difference between being two feet long and two feet short is four feet, but only one of those putts has a chance of going in. The ideal putt is aimed to be 18 inches past the hole. Most golfers miss putts short. A putt that doesn't make the hole has no chance of going in. There's nothing worse than a putt on a perfect line that stops a roll or two shot. An easy shot wasted.

I think you should take an aggressive stance when putting. By an aggressive stance, I mean a stance that makes you feel that you are ready to smack the ball into the hole. Baseball players take a aggressive stance when they are ready to bat.

Hone your putting skills until you *believe* that you can make any four footer. Once you *believe* this, you won't care if you go a bit past the hole on your first putt.

Tell yourself you are the best putter in the world. It doesn't matter whether you are or you aren't. Tell yourself that you are

Somebody's got to be the best putter in the world.

Why not you?

Before you putt, it is important that you stare at the ball and the hole, and imagine the ball going into the hole. I recommend *not* taking a practice stroke once you take your stance. In other words, look at the ball and hole, imagine the ball going into the hole, walk up to your ball, put your putter down square, take your stance, draw the putter back deliberately keeping the blade square to your line, and hit the putt firmly with the resolve that it is going into the cup.

45

MUST SHOTS

There are some shots that you must learn, but they are all easy. Here they are:

1.   Bunker shot.

2.   Chip shot.

3.   Short lob wedge.

4.   Longer, but less than full, sand wedge pitch shot.

5.   Full pitch shot.

These are THE SCORING SHOTS.
You must learn them and practice them.
When you do, your scores will drop.
Dramatically.

46

CHIPPING PRACTICE

R emember when we played at Glen Abbey?

I never forget you chipped in on the first hole to go one under. Then after two pars, you birdied the fourth to go two under. The guys that we were with asked you if *you* were a pro.

Do you remember why you chip so well that day?

You tol' me that it was because you played a game in your backyard that I had showed you. Remember?

You get a laundry basket, pail or a garbage can, and chip at it from various distances. Score one point for a hit and two points if you get it inside. Use your wedges, your 9-iron and 8-iron to get the feel for all of them.

I remember another day that you chipped well too and it was right after I showed you another chipping drill. I tol' you that when you practice your chips, try to sink the chip.

I tol' you to stay on the practice green until you sunk three chips. I remember one day you stayed there for over an hour. (The good thing about trying to sink the chip is that it trains your automatic golfer to do this automatically.)

I remember the first time that you practiced this way before a club match, you chipped in on the 18th hole to win the match!

47

VIDEOTAPING:
WHAT ARE YOU DOING RIGHT?

I bet that most golf teachers use videotape to point out what you are doing wrong. That make no sense.

Juan, promise me this - that you only videotape yourself when you are hitting the ball well. Play the tape over and over until you can see in your mind what your body looks like when you hit the ball well.

48

MAKE LOVE
TO YOUR GOLF COURSE

Juan, do you love your wife?

I know you do and you tol' me that you think she is the most beautiful woman in the world.

As far as I am concerned, a golf course is the most beautiful place on earth. I think this is one reason why people like to golf. Think of your golf course like your wife. Make love to your golf course.

Stare at it. Savour it. Smell it. Touch it. Dream about it. Protect it. Talk to it. Know it up and down, inside and out, backwards and forwards

Explore every nook and cranny. Surprise it. Caress it. Draw pictures of it. Know where it can be troublesome.

Respect it Honour it. Love it.

Make love to your golf course.

49

TRY WALKING YOUR COURSE GREEN TO TEE

It wasn't such a long time ago that golf courses were simply parks or public land. Golfers were required to wear red coats to warn those who were taking a walk in the park that a golfer was playing in their vicinity.

Times have changed and on most golf courses you can't just go for a walk, but I know that you like to play early in the morning or in the late afternoon. Try this one day. Just like I tell you to practice, green to tee, *walk your course green to tee.* Walk your course from the 18th green to the first tee. Imagine what your shots look like coming at you and plan your game from the green to the tee.

I bet you, Juan, that the proper way to play the hole jumps out at you. I bet you that you will see that the holes are easier than they look the other way around.

Play your next round in your mind as you are falling asleep, imagining the hole from green to tee.

50

MAKE YOUR OWN
COURSE BOOK

I remember you did this many years ago and I thought it was a good idea, but not for the reasons you thought it was a good idea.

I remember you bought a small notebook that you could carry in your pocket and then you went to every hole and recorded every marked sprinkler head, sketched every green and paced off its size. You thought this was a good idea because you had your own course book. *I thought it was a good idea because it made you more aware of the golf course.* You learned, for 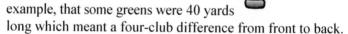 example, that some greens were 40 yards long which meant a four-club difference from front to back.

I remember that you also kept a notebook in your locker and you kept track of every round, hole by hole, noting your score in relation to par. You came to me one day and tol' me that over the year you had birdied every hole on the course at some time. I think you learned something about the game of golf when you saw that.

51

THE RULES

The Rules of Golf are the rules of golf.

Once you tee up your ball at the first hole, you are agreeing to play by a certain set of rules: The Rules Of Golf.

If you don't know the rules of the game, how can you play by the rules?

Do you know what "loose impediments" are? Do you know what an "obstruction" is? Do you know what relief you can take in certain situations? Do you know what "through the green" and "closely mown area" mean?

Players are not permitted to agree to exclude the operation of any rule or to waive any penalty. If you do this in a tournament, you will be disqualified.

In match play, the concession of a stroke, hole or match may not be declined or waived.

Even the Committee [either the committee in charge of a specific competition or the committee in charge of the course] is not permitted to waive the rules although the Committee make what are known as "local rules" for abnormal conditions and other situations which are described in an appendix to the Rules.

Always check for local rules in effect. They can save you strokes. Otherwise, a golfer is expected to play by the rules and, likewise, has the expectation that all others will as well.

Now in a friendly game, who really cares? So, for example, let's say that you go out to a public course and join a threesome of guys put together by the starter to form a foursome and who are not playing any sort of a match. What you don't want to do in these circumstances is call them, let's say for carrying too many clubs. Who really cares?

On the other hand, if you are in a meaningful match where there is something at stake, the rule is that all players are expected to play by the rules. All of the rules.

In order to play by the rules one has to know the rules. Do you? Are you sure?

There is an easy solution to this simple problem. Buy this year's rule book and read it. The Rules of Golf change from time to time, so last year's book may or may not be complete.

Golf is an honourable game. This is one of the first things that I taught you. Sometimes, for example, you hit the ball twice and you are the only one who knows. You must call penalty on yourself.

52
THERE'S MORE THAN ONE WAY TO PLAY A HOLE

It's so important to know all of the rules because you can use them to your advantage. Sometimes, if you don't know the rules, it can cost you strokes.

So, Juan, do you remember the tournament when you played with your friend Brian? How is he? Say hello to him, will you?.

It was a two-day tournament and, after the first day, you guys weren't doing so good. The next day you guys were on fire and you needed a par on the last hole to finish all the way up to second. You stepped up to the ball and hooked it so far that you went on the other fairway. But, Juan, you did a smart thing. You play up that fairway and then over a big tree to get on the green in regulation and par the hole.

A golfer who didn't know that you can play on another fairway might have wasted a shot to get back on the proper fairway.

53

TOURNAMENT MATCH PLAY

Match play is what golf competition is all about. It's a beautiful blend of *skill, psychology, control, and strategy.*

A golf match is exciting, *but so is war*! And a golf match is like a war. Face-to-face with the enemy. Last man standing wins.

Some matches are a slaughter. Sometimes it comes down to the last putt on the last hole. You never know how it's going to turn out until it's over, so all you can do is *give yourself the best opportunity to win. Be there, so that when the door opens, you can walk through.*

So, Juan, how can you do this?

The most important thing that I can tell you is that you have to be prepared mentally and emotionally. Once you're in the competition, it's too late to improve your skills. *You've got to go with what you got.* But the best skills won't help if you don't use them properly.

Lesser skilled golfers have won many matches. How do you explain that?

Winning a golf match is a combination of skill, psychology, control, and strategy.

54

HANG TOUGH AND STEADY

Just like the winds of war shift, the advantage in a golf match can shift with every shot. Up and down like a roller coaster ride. *You have to be prepared to ride the roller coaster if you want to win the match.*

How do you do this? *Hang tough and steady.*

One thing that can drive a golfer crazy is an opponent that just keeps on coming.

Always be there, in play, ready to strike. Keep the ball in play. Steady and relentless.

Keeping the ball in play and out of trouble puts tremendous pressure on your opponent to make an amazing shot. Good. That's what you want him to feel. Let him make the tough decisions. Let him make the mistake.

Every time your opponent sees your ball in play and you ready to strike, it makes him anxious. It makes him think about *your* shot. He starts thinking "what ifs" rather than thinking about His shot. He starts feeling the pressure to keep even with you.

He starts taking chances, and that's what you want.

You know that in a golf match, you play the course, not the opponent, but if your opponent get anxious enough, he will forget this and when he does, you are on your way to victory.

55

BE EMOTIONALLY NEUTRAL

*S*tay *as emotionally steady, unemotional as you can.*

Why?

Because the emotional roller coaster ride is tiring and it can affect the decisions that you make. If you celebrate your successes, sure you get pumped, but it means that you've got farther to fall when your opponent gains the advantage. *It's the emotional impact of feeling down that you must guard against.* That sinking feeling you get from falling from an emotional height is dangerous in a golf match.

If you feel down, or relatively down, you are more likely to experience fear, anxiety, despair, discouragement and even panic at the critical moments in a match. However, if you are neutral emotionally, then you don't have to worry. *You are protected.*

Being neutral emotionally means reacting the same way, neutrally, whether you chip in for an eagle or miss a six-inch putt. You accept completely whatever happens as just another event on the way to you winning the match.

The only exception is when you sense that your opponent is down emotionally. Now is the time when you can use a display of emotion *as a weapon.* If you make an amazing shot that by itself 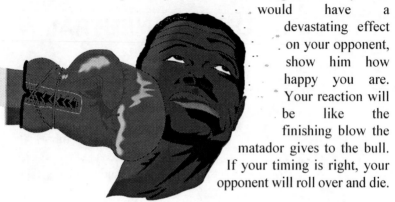 would have a devastating effect on your opponent, show him how happy you are. Your reaction will be like the finishing blow the matador gives to the bull. If your timing is right, your opponent will roll over and die.

When he does that, be prepared to receive una oreja.

56

DOMINATE YOUR OPPONENT

Even if your opponent has more guns, you can win if you break his spirit.

Dominate your opponent as the matador dominates the bull, with knowledge and skill.

Wear him down so he is *aplamado*, heavy and tired, like the bull waiting to be killed. To do this you must be in shape mentally and physically.

In most cases, your opponent is going to be nervous or over-confident. Either way, it doesn't matter. Use it to your advantage.

To break his spirit, you have to get him to be afraid or confused.

Start in on him even before the match begins. You shake your opponent's hand, wish him luck, and then you don't talk to him the rest of the round. You are not being rude. You have got much more on your mind than chit-chat (did I say that right, chit-chat?).

You don't want anything to distract you from your number one thought, which is getting the ball into the hole in the least number of strokes, and you want your opponent to be alone with his thoughts.

You know what to do about the mental game. Does he?

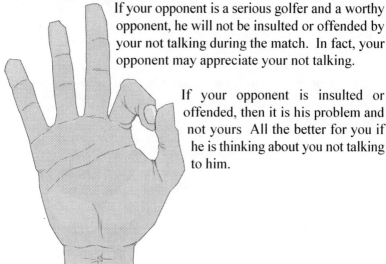

If your opponent is a serious golfer and a worthy opponent, he will not be insulted or offended by your not talking during the match. In fact, your opponent may appreciate your not talking.

If your opponent is insulted or offended, then it is his problem and not yours All the better for you if he is thinking about you not talking to him.

57

IT'S OVER WHEN IT'S OVER:
NOT UNTIL

Y ou can't predict the future.

[Why did you have to tell me that, Frank?]

You never know what's going to happen. A golf match is never over until it's over.

I remember two times you tell me about when big leads were over-come.

You were two down with four to go in a doubles match and your partner was playing so poorly that he almost walked off the course. But your team went birdie, par, par, par to win three of the next four holes and take the match.

I also remember the time you were up six and seven and lost!

*You never know
what is going to happen in a match.*

58

GO WITH WHAT GOT YOU THERE

S ometimes I see golfers changing something about their game
on the range before a match in the club
championship.

Juan, if you qualify for the club championship
tournament, then you must be doing something
right.

Resist any temptation to try something
different.

Go with what got you there.

59

PLAY GOOD ENOUGH TO WIN

Remember that in match play, the object of this game is to get the ball into the hole in fewer strokes than your opponent. This is a bit different than when you are playing for score.

You only need to play good enough to win.

X-cellent

So, for example, if you need only to two-putt to win the hole, make sure that you two-putt. There's no reason to sink the first putt. Make sure that first putt is "gimme close".

60

YOU ARE YOUR ONLY FRIEND

When you are in a match, you are your only friend. So, *be a good friend to yourself.* Give yourself encouragement. Always be positive and only positive.

Have some easy sayings or phrases that you can use to get yourself back into focus if you find yourself drifting.

Juan, I been telling you things about golf for 20 years. Surely you can remember some of those things that I tol' you!

How 'bout: Golf is just a game; a game of inches. But, it's as much a game of inches for your opponent, as it is for you. Nothing always goes your way. If your opponent is getting the breaks, it only means that you are due to get yours. Be ready when opportunity presents itself.

Here's even a better one:

Someone is going to be champion. It might as well be you.

61

FORGET THE SCORE

A golf match is played one shot at a time. So be there, right there on every shot. Totally absorbed in the shot.

There are so many things waiting to distract you, but if you are immersed in the process of your shot, you can't possibly be distracted.

Perhaps one of the worst distractions is thinking about the score. It's OK to be *aware* of how you stand on a hole and in the match. In fact, it's important to be *aware* of how you stand, but that's all. Once you start *thinking* about the score, your attention is diverted to the past and the future instead of being focused on the present.

You think *"I only need..", "If I lose this hole...," "If I hadn't..., then I would have been...".* None of these thoughts can help you, only hurt you.

So, what do you do when you find yourself thinking about the score? Simply reabsorb yourself in your next shot.

By the way, let your opponent keep score. You know that thinking about the score can distract you from playing one shot at a time. Give your opponent at least 17 chances to let the score distract him from his shot.

62

TOURNAMENT MEDAL PLAY

*H*ow you think a matador would play a medal play golf tournament?

The matador knows that when he faces the bull, he can't afford to make a mistake. So, the matador fights the bull carefully and deliberately. In a medal play golf tournament, it is important for you to play cautiously, well within your ability level, keeping the ball in play and not making a mistake that will kill your chances of winning the tournament.

Occasionally, you may "go for it", and that's OK where you don't risk losing a ball, going out of bounds or incurring some penalty which will cost you strokes and your resolve. Otherwise, play the highest percentage shot, even sometimes where it costs you a shot, as protection against getting into trouble and losing two or three.

The matador always knows how his opponent, the bull, is doing. In a medal play tournament, *you never know* how the rest of the field is doing. For example, you may think that the elements are hurting your score and you may think that you are out of the tournament, but remember: all of your competitors are playing under the same conditions.

In every tournament, there is a second-place finisher who walks away from the score board thinking "If I had only...".

63

WIN OR LOSE: LIKE A MAN

Sometimes in a tournament match, if you don't talk to your opponent the whole round and then you win, your opponent will be angry at you. Don't you worry, because your opponent is really angry at himself.

I tell you one thing however, Juan. Always be fair. Play by the rules and *win or lose like a man,* which means enjoy the competition and accept the result with grace.

Some players try to do things purposefully to distract or annoy you. If this happens, Juan, point out to your opponent what he did and ask whether he realized he had done it. Step back from your shot, get refocused, and hit the best shot of the day. He won't do it again.

If your opponent calls you for a rule infraction, don't be angry with your opponent. It's not your opponent's fault that you broke the rules. You should and must call yourself if you are aware of any rule infraction that you have committed. That's how golf has been played for hundreds of years.

A game of honour.

64

GET YOUR BUTTERFLIES FLYING IN FORMATION

I n any golfing competition, it's normal and actually desirable to feel excited with anticipation. The trick is to harness that energy. Somebody tol' me this in different words. He said:

"It's OK to have butterflies. Just get them flying in formation!"

Relaxed or nervous are not really what you want to be. Somewhere in between. Calmly disturbed, alertly absorbed, attentively interested or cooly agitated are better ways to describe how you want to feel.

It's that uneasy nervous feeling that makes competition exciting.

65

THE ZONE

There's a special place where you want to be when you are playing an important match. Most people call it "the zone."

The zone is a place of intense and concentrated focus. It's a place where the energy of passion, fear and enthusiasm is transformed into strength and singularity of purpose.

The zone is a quiet place with nothing going on but your calmness and confidence. You don't have to rush or hurry here because everything and everyone waits for you. Time runs according to *your* watch and *your* wishes.

You feel confident and everything about you shows this confidence. You stand tall and straight and you walk slowly because you have complete command of everything in this place. You feel like there is a light on you as you walk down the course. Not a bright light, but just a bit brighter and clearer than anywhere else.

Everyone and everything else is scenery.

Even though it sounds like the zone is far away from your everyday existence, it's really just another level of consciousness that's quite easy to reach.

It's like taking an elevator
one floor down
to a deeper level of consciousness.

Go there and stay there sometime prior to your pre-round practice. I suggest that you go there no more than 30 to 45 minutes before you tee off.

There are people who exist naturally in the zone. Most of us need to learn how to get there. Getting fully into the zone is a process.

If you want to play in the zone, the first thing that you must do is to *make the conscious decision* that you want to go to the zone. The next thing that you should do is to listen to this tape or read some notes that you make about your personal experiences in the zone. This will reinforce your decision that you want to be in the zone and will start to get you focused.

When you are ready, get your clubs and do some putting and chipping. Remind yourself that these are skills that you will need today to score. You can go hit a few balls at the driving range if you like, but your objective is merely to loosen your muscles and to get your body in sync with your mind.

When you are finished, go to the tee. As you wait for your opponent, hit a few lob wedge or sand wedge shots. These are shots that you will need today, so focus on the mechanics of hitting them well. Be on the tee on time, waiting for your opponent, but be immersed in your little lob wedge game.

If you prefer, you can carry your own clubs. This way you can be by yourself and walk slowly at your own pace. Also, carrying your clubs keeps you relaxed and loose because it tires your muscles out a bit. Walking slowly will also calm you down and will get your body into the right rhythm for golf, which is a relaxed, but purposeful rhythm.

If you take a caddy, get your own. Don't ever ride in a cart with your opponent. Make your opponent wait for you. You don't do anything until you are 100% ready.

Everyone and everything waits for you as you quietly and methodically go about your business.

When you see your opponent, shake hands, say "good luck", and  that's it for the talking for the rest of the match. You have got work to do and if your opponent doesn't realize it, all the better for you.

It appears as if you don't have any emotions. Whatever happens, you accept it with the same reaction. No reaction.

You know that celebrating your success and getting down on yourself about your mistakes is a formula for defeat. So, when you 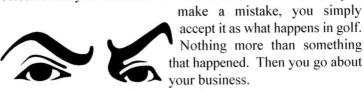 make a mistake, you simply accept it as what happens in golf. Nothing more than something that happened. Then you go about your business.

You know that getting angry at yourself for making a mistake leads to fear of doing it again. Fear is distracting and debilitating.

You are patient as you prepare for your shot and as others prepare for theirs. You may have a slight scowl on your face, but that is an expression of calm determination. When you are in a state of calm determination, your face naturally goes into this expression.

Others recognize it subconsciously as one of calm determination.

You understand that you can make a mistake and still succeed.

You are not in a hurry to do anything. You walk with a purposeful saunter. As you walk down the fairway, each step you take is deliberate and says,

"I'm in charge here, thank you for coming today and partaking in my golf match with you."

You go through your pre-shot routine for each type of shot religiously.

You are a machine, a golfing machine, not a person, and your sole purpose is to win the match. Nothing is going to interfere with that objective and nothing does. Nothing is going to phase you and nothing does.

Relentless and steady. Confident. Assured. Poised. Decisive. Stone-cold steel.

As you are walking to the tee, up the fairway or to the green, you are thinking about the shot that you will make, assessing the factors that may affect your shot and then actually seeing it happen.

As you walk you are also aware of the beauty of the surroundings, the sun, the clouds, the trees, the birds, the beauty of nature. You are thankful that you have the opportunity to be alive, to play golf, and to compete in this match.

If you make a bad shot, so what? You come back with an amazing shot. If you lose a hole, so what? You will come back. And you do, because this is your special place and you are in charge.

You are aware of the score, but you don't dwell on it. The score is what it is. *The only thing that you can do about the score is to play the best golf that you can possibly play.* If you do this, the score will still be what it is.

You are *confident* that you will win the match and you realize that most matches are close and are not over until the last few holes. Some come down to the 18th hole or go into sudden death. So what?

You are *confident* that you will win all of the matches, even the close ones.

A champion must win all of the matches, even the close ones.

Someone will win all of the matches. It might as well be you.

Someone will be champion. It might as well be you.

You understand that the winning difference in a close match can be one thought.

One thought!

You know that when you are playing against an opponent, your opponent will be nervous and unsure of himself because that is what happens to most people, especially when they are in a place that is foreign to them or with someone who makes them nervous.

Golfing machines make human golfers nervous.

As your opponent crumbles and makes poor shots, you show no emotion. You expect your opponent to make poor shots and so it doesn't surprise you or delight you.

When your opponent makes a good shot, you are neither surprised nor disappointed. It just is what is happening at the moment, which is all normal for a golf match. It just doesn't matter because all that you are concerned with is going about your business of winning the match. All you are thinking about is what you have to do at that moment. That is your business for the day. What you have to do at that moment.

You are there for every shot. Right there.
Totally absorbed in that shot.

It appears to your opponents that you make decisions quickly and decisively. For example, if your opponent makes a good first putt and is within gimme range early in the match, give the putt quickly and decisively.

Order your opponent to "take it".

You know that you make your decisions decisively and confidently, but not until you are ready.

You are never afraid to change your mind, even if you have already set up to the ball. You may even try this on purpose just to show your opponent that you will not take your shot until you are perfectly ready to do so.

If your opponent compliments you on a good shot, that is his choice. Be polite and say thank you, but there is no need to return the compliment, nor to compliment your opponent on any shot. Complimenting an opponent on a shot shows that you are paying attention and that you care about the shot. You couldn't care less about your opponent's shot, or at least you don't show it.

You are relentlessly confident.

You know what your job is and you are simply executing the plan, one shot at a time.

When you stand up to the tee, you pick a spot in the distance and then you hit the ball with the confidence that you will hit the ball there.

When you are getting ready to putt, you are staring at your ball and imagining the path that your ball will take on its way into the hole. As you look, you will see a pathway seem to form on the green. Sometimes it may appear as if it's a highway with light standards, just waiting for you to putt the ball down it, into the hole.

Before every shot, you give your mind a chance to lock into your target.

You are powerful, but it appears to your opponent that your power is effortless.

Easy, graceful, simple, smooth power.

You don't mark your score until well after your opponent does and never before you are standing on the next tee. The score is really irrelevant because you know you are going to win.

If you win the match, you are pleased, but not elated. You will thank your opponent for being a worthy adversary, for partaking in the match, and you will compliment him on the highlights of his round.

If your opponent wins the match, you would rather have won, you may be mildly disappointed, but you will thank your opponent for being a worthy adversary, for partaking in the match, and you will compliment him on the highlights of his round. *You are comforted with the knowledge that there is no such thing as defeat. Only preparation for a greater day.*

Now here's the secret, Juan: *Getting to and staying in the zone is a skill that needs to be practiced to be effective.*

Practice it every round that you play and watch what happens.

66

BE HAPPY, JUAN

Juan, as you listen to this tape, I know you are sad that I am dead. The only thing I can tell you is that I have lived a good life. I have really enjoyed my life and I was very fortunate.

Be happy to be alive, Juan. Be happy to have the opportunity to do whatever you want to do. Be happy to be with your family and friends.

I will be there with you on the course. When you make a birdie, when you chip in, when you sink a long putt, I'll be there with you. Look over your shoulder. Look in a tree. Look in the sky. I'll be there.

I give you my red and white golf bag with my name on it. Juan, promise me that when you compete for a championship, and you will some day, you will use my bag so that I can be there with you. Your opponents may think it's unfair: two against one.

But really Juan, how much help can a dead golf pro give you? That's up to you, my friend!

Play excellent golf, and enjoy every minute of your life.

Act like a champion all of the time

and you will be a champion.

FRANCISCO (FRANK) LOPEZ

Frank Lopez was a great golf teacher.

Born in Spain in 1945, young Frank learned to play golf as a caddy at the Real Club de Golf in Prat de Llobragat, a suburb of Barcelona. Traveling to North America as a teenager in search of golfing opportunities, he worked first in Glen Ridge Country Club in New Jersey, and then settled in Toronto in 1969, working at Rosedale Golf Club, Oakdale Golf and Country Club and Streetsville Glen Golf Club.

Educated in life, Frank had a deep insight into the psychology of the human mind. Frank understood instinctively that an image was worth a 1000 words of instruction and therefore would tell students to "stand tall, be proud like a matador and hit it", rather than getting into the intricate and confusing details of the sequential bending, twisting and straightening various body parts.

He died April 9, 1992 at the age of 47.

JONATHAN FINE

Jonathan Fine is the senior partner of the Toronto law firm Fine & Deo and is recognized nationally as a leading litigator in the field of Condominium Law. In addition to practicing and teaching law for over 20 years, Mr. Fine has contributed articles to various publications and hosted live television talk-shows originating out of Toronto.

Mr. Fine has also been a student of motivation and success and created the personal development seminar *Stand Tall, Be Proud and Hit It*. He lives in Toronto with his wife Shelley and four children.

"This book is the very best golf book that I have ever read...The best thing about the golf teachings in this book is that they really work.... an immediate and most profound impact on my game.... my scores dropped immediately!"

                    -Steve Justein, Tournament Chairman,
                    Oakdale Golf & Country Club,
                    Toronto, Ontario.

"Finally a golf book that I could read from cover to cover...straight forward, to the point. The book is not about quick fixes or gimmicks; its about human behaviour"

                    -Joshua H. Cooper, Director,
                    Par Golf Camps Inc.
                    Toronto Maccabi Golf Coach

"A fascinating book. I couldn't put it down."

                    -Aron Rock, Teaching Professional,
                    Uplands Golf Club, Toronto, Ontario

"Chapter 65: 'The Zone' is a must read for ANY athlete competing in ANY sport!"

                    -Jesse Dylan,
                    Team Canada Triathlete

"After reading "Golf is a Very Simple Game" golfers should see a marked improvement not only in their scores but also in their appreciation of the game"

                    -Tim McKeown
                    Golf writer